The Flowers That Softly Spoke

DEE RUSSELL

Inspiring Voices books may be ordered through booksellers or by contacting:

Inspiring Voices
1663 Liberty Drive
Bloomington, IN 47403
www.inspiringvoices.com
1 (866) 697-5313

ISBN: 978-1-4624-1104-7 (sc)
ISBN: 978-1-4624-1105-4 (e)

Print information available on the last page.

Inspiring Voices rev. date: 08/11/2015

InspiringVoices®

The Flowers That Softly Spoke

DEE RUSSELL

To those who take the time to stop and smell the roses and appreciate nature as one of God's ways of providing an understanding of the many aspects of this life.

Walk into my world.
Share a bit of you.
Tell me of your pleasures, your hopes,
your dreams, your view.

Walk into my day, share with me
some plans.
Let's enjoy a bit of fellowship
And make life a bit more grand.

Share with me your laughter.
Share with me your pain.
Maybe just the two of us can right the
wrong again.

Have a spot of friendliness.
Share a crumb of care.
Let's walk into tomorrow
And find some beauty there.

Table of Contents

Introduction

Do you believe that flowers speak?
You may smile a bit at the thought and reply, "Yes, flowers sometimes
nod in the soft summer breeze, but speak? Well, hardly."
But wait!

In soft whispers and nudges through different seasons of my life—being a wife, raising a family, and fulfilling my place in our community—God has sometimes used the quietness of nature and the life of these colorful plants to speak, teaching valuable lessons that I sorely needed to learn.

My flower garden is one of my favorite places to be. There as I work, planting, weeding, and caring tenderly for each plant, I experience the majestic orchestration of nature demonstrated through birth, growth, climax, and even the bittersweet taste of death, but always a hope of resurrection.

Just as there are seasons in nature, there are seasons of life, and we can experience a steadfast faithfulness even in the winters of our lives and know it all works together for our Creator's purposes.

My experiences teach me also that sometimes flowers have magical messages. They have driven a point home when I just couldn't seem to get it. You will find intermingled within these pages the stories that they tell of

- *relationships,* as life unfolds through interaction with others;
- *growth and opportunities* that expand our being so that we can make positive contributions to the world;
- *perseverance,* which calls us to deal with situations that might not be our choosing but nourish us to greater stability and attainment when we have stood the test; and

- *hope* in the redemptive power of tomorrow, whether in this life or in the next.

Jesus pointed to the lilies of the field, the birds of the air, and the grass of the field, when instructing on attitudes toward life and sustenance. We must not worry but seek the face of God and His righteousness, we are told, and all things shall be added to us (Matthew 6:28–33). We can willfully go about making our own decisions regarding the life we lead, or we can choose the higher calling of listening to the still small voice within and searching out the wisdom of the scriptures that call us to a better way. When we do, our path leads us to a future where God's faithfulness is always fulfilled.

Relationships

The years teach much
which the days
never know.
—Ralph Waldo Emerson

Lilacs

I tenderly stroked the velvety beard of the lush iris a neighbor had just given me. It was one of the several varieties she had generously divided when I had commented on her iris bed when visiting her home as a community volunteer for the Heart Fund.

"Now place the different varieties separately in your garden," she said. "Give them room to grow. You will have a wealth of color for years to come. Just remember, some varieties are of weaker stock than others. They will need a little more loving care. Get a nice instruction manual and follow the directions for plush continual blooms of *all* varieties year after year." I hurried home, eager to place the plants in just the right spot for each color. I purchased a guide and was soon on my way to growing my own lovely iris bed.

Through the years, I thought of my generous friend as my iris bed greeted me in full color each spring. But after a while, I noticed with much trepidation that many of the clumps had turned to pale lavender, and the rich colors that had once graced my garden were a faded memory. Had I been giving them the attention they had received in the years I first acquired them? No. I realized I had not. I had taken their generous blooms too much for granted without maintaining their needed care and nurturing.

Relationships also need to be nurtured with our love and care. Yet there are some relationships that clearly are not to our benefit and will have a negative impact. These should be allowed to fade away. But many of our relationships—with those who love and affirm us, or whom we are meant to love and affirm—need nurturing. Perhaps we can do this through an unexpected phone call, a note of appreciation, or other gestures of affirmation. When we take the time for tender nurturing of friendships too, we continue to enjoy their splendor.

Delphinium Delight

I stood back to admire my beautiful, stately bouquet of delphiniums. How gorgeous the deep purple and lavender stalks looked as they loomed upward from the crystal vase! The first blooms of the season were so enjoyable, adorning my dining-room table.

I marveled at their brilliance, chiding myself of a miracle that I could assist in producing such blooms from my sometimes not-so-green thumb.

Then I recalled an adage told to me by an elderly neighbor a few years back: "Flowers will bloom longer and brighter when given as a gift, if the giver gives in love and sincerity."

As an inspiration for my daughter's birthday in March, I sent her delphinium bulbs for her flower garden. When we came back from our tropical home to our Indiana farm in May, I found she had divided the bulbs in half—providing some for my garden too. My gift had been returned, rich and plentiful, and I was blessed throughout my summer days with their fragrance and beauty.

> Cast your bread upon the waters,
> for after many days,
> you will find it again.
>
> Ecclesiastes 11:1

Angels Sent from God

When special people come to mind,
I always pause a while,
Remembering all those moments
That are sure to bring a smile.

When I was down,
you were there
With quiet sympathy,
Lending me that helping hand
To prod my destiny.

The happy days
When dreams once dreamed
Were suddenly realized,
You bounced right in my world with glee,
Sharing my delight.

The little note that came one day
When darkness had stepped in,
Assured me that rainbows
Would flood my life again.

You always seem to know just when
To add a touch of you.
To light my world in a special way
Like a rainbow's sudden hue.

So today my pleasure must be shared;
You're the one who gets the nod.
For special people such as you
Are surely angels sent from God.

A friend is dearer than the light of heaven;
For it would be better for us that the sun were extinguished
Than that we should be without friends.

—St. Chrysostom

Unspoken Friendship

She slipped into my studio almost unnoticed—very polite, very refined.

A slight bit of a lady with a shy demeanor and sweet smile—somewhere in her late fifties, perhaps. The dark features of her Japanese ancestry told of her family and her loyalties.

After bowing deftly, she found the seat that I motioned for her to take. She couldn't speak English, but she was there to learn. I had explained earlier to her daughter, when asked about English language lessons for her that we didn't usually teach language in our music and art studio in Hawaii but I would share what I could.

Mieko had come to the island from Japan to help with the care of a five-year-old grandson, and I sensed that being far from home with little knowledge of our culture was hard for her. So a date was set for instruction, and we parted. I was genuinely glad to embark on this adventure together.

Beginning with colors and pointing to each one, I explained: *aka* is red, *midor* is green, *ki* is yellow, *auro* is blue. A quick learner, we soon progressed to numbers and the art of counting change. The JCPenney catalog was helpful for Mieko to relate her world to the names we had for the same items in America. We laughed together at my attempts to help and her struggles to achieve; it was great fun.

Mieko could understand more than she could speak, so to help her become fluent, I insisted that she form complete sentences. Sometimes I would point out items in the studio and use them as nouns for simple sentences. Throughout our lessons, she was gracious and conscientious—a real delight to work with.

"Now we're going to the mini-mall," I announced when Mieko became more adept in speaking short sentences. Together we entered a women's boutique and, being the women of fashion that we were, compared purses, admired jewelry, and giggled at bikinis we no longer cared to wear. Walking back to the studio, Mieko pointed out and named the flowering trees the Hawaiian islands had in common with Japan. It was a special time of togetherness, although no long sentences were spoken. Before leaving that day, she thanked me over and over—*Arigatou gozaimasu, arigatou gozaimasu*—then bowed gracefully and left.

At the close of our three-month series of English lessons, she pointed at the calendar to show me the date at the end of the month when she would be leaving for Japan. She had only come for four months to be with her daughter and grandson, and her visa would soon be up.

Before leaving, she came with a tiny teapot and Japanese delicacies as a farewell gift. I was so thrilled by her kindness that I mistakenly tried to give her a hug. She quickly stepped back, bowed slightly, and left.

I missed our times together and sent, by way of her daughter's visit to Japan, a painting I had finished of the teapot she had given me. Mieko came back the next year and the next. We enjoyed each other's company as she gained proficiency in the English language.

On her last visit, she stated that she wanted to take art lessons. She could now use her newly acquired language to describe the colors on her palette. The time was to end too soon, for one day she told me she would be leaving again.

On a day near her departure, she appeared again with Japanese delicacies. I thanked her warmly for her many kindnesses to me.

I knew I had arrived when she paused before she left, then came back to give me a hug.

A friend may well be reckoned
the masterpiece of nature.

—Ralph Waldo Emerson

The Healing of Laughter

We started jauntily on our way, just the three of us, friends for years who had weathered many storms together. What could have been a depressing expedition was not. You see, we were to go to a cancer clinic. My friend Hallie had been told earlier that she had a very large growth in her breast. Surgery had removed it, and today she was to set up treatments for the strongest chemo that her body could manage.

Renee and I were going with her for moral support. Hallie, however, would not be daunted by the severity of it all. No, everything was funny to her as we rode along. Renee was known for her laughter, so she laughed along with her and I, too, joined in.

We entered the clinic, and Hallie asked if we could go in with her to the examining room. The jokes and laughter continued. I saw the attendant glancing curiously at us from time to time. I'm sure she was thinking, *Are these people for real?*

Hallie's emerging philosophy seemed to convey this: The future cannot spoil the pleasure of today with my friends. We will seize the moments and enjoy the time God has given.

In the months ahead, Halle got through the severe treatments, refusing to have a negative attitude. I'm sure she had her days, but she chose to latch on to faith, embracing each day with constructive living.

As the months progressed, she lost all her hair, but donned a stylish salt-and-pepper wig to maintain a perspective of who she was. One day, she suggested I attend a church conference with her in a city about sixty miles away. On the way home, we spotted a youth of about eighteen sitting along the road in an old pickup truck, selling bunches of roses. On investigation, we found he had only a few left, and they had been marked down considerably.

"Oh, Hallie, that's a reasonable price," I said. "And they are so beautiful. Let's stop and help him out."

"Yes, let's do. I would love some," she replied enthusiastically. So we stopped and strode over to his pickup truck.

I selected my favorite, pink, and she chose sunny yellow. Just as Hallie opened her purse to pay for her purchase, a gust of wind caught her wig, and it went rolling down the side of the highway. Soon she was scampering after it, her baldness from the chemo treatments exposed.

I looked at the young man and shrugged. He didn't say a word, and I can't describe the look on his face. Returning finally after retrieving her rolling hairpiece, Hallie plopped it back on her head and held it down as she paid for her roses. We then marched to our car spritely to keep our dignity. Only later, when we were out of sight, did we convulse in laughter.

That was many years ago, and Hallie has been cancer-free since. There could be many factors why the cancer did not return, but one of the main ones surely was Hallie's ability to cast her care and destiny on the Higher Power, leaving it there to make the most of the days given to her.

A cheerful heart is good medicine, *but a crushed spirit dries up the bones.*
Proverbs 17:22

Don't walk behind me: I may not lead.
Don't walk in front of me; I may not follow.
Just walk beside me and be my friend.
—Albert Camus

13

Relationships: A Valuable Teacher

Our interactions with others can teach some of life's valuable lessons. However, when our relationships aren't working, it might be time for self-examination as well as forgiveness of others and ourselves. Even in this, we can be refined and enlarged, for we must admit that even a negative person or situation can be the teacher of lessons.

When we begin to acknowledge that all people, including ourselves, are prone to blunders but created for a purpose on this earth, we can have a greater respect for others on life's pathway.

There is a wonderful formula for friendship, for it is the description of the Father's response to us when we ask for wisdom: "He is pure and peace loving, considerate, submissive, full of mercy and good fruit, impartial and sincere" (James 3:17–18).

What a message! We are then told that those who sow in peace raise a harvest of righteousness. What a promise!

Sly Slips

"How could she do that?" I ranted, twirling around from the kitchen sink. "She knew I wanted to help. She purposely left me out!" After saddling the dish towel over the towel rack, I pranced into the nursery, swung baby Laura from the crib, and returned to find a bottle in the refrigerator to sooth her crying.

"Maybe she didn't realize you'd feel left out," offered Carla, my next-door neighbor, as we finished our morning coffee.

"But everyone else has been asked to help with the reception."

"Don't be upset," she offered gently. "You mustn't carry your feelings around on your shoulders. They could get pretty heavy, you know."

I mellowed somewhat. "You're right, of course. I do let things bother me too much."

Carla smiled and left.

Slumping into a chair, I held my baby daughter carefully as I playful rubbed her gentle skin. I mused at how we girls had gone through school together and attended the usual parties and gab sessions. Now Marci was to be married and would leave the community.

Her reception would be very small, with friends pitching in to help with the cake and decorations. Of course we were invited to the wedding and would go, but a twinge of hurt dug at me that I hadn't been included in the reception planning as most of the other girls had. Marci and I had sometimes had our differences, but …

Well, I would just call and ask if they needed help. I knew my pity party was ridiculous. Perhaps she could use my matching crystal goblets. They were so exquisite for special occasions. I would fashion bouquets from the garden at my back door. Everyone knew I had a knack for making flower arrangements. They would be perfect for the setting: a little country church.

"Why, how nice to hear from you," Marci purred.

I told her about the goblets and the arrangements I could make, if needed. "Do you have any bouquets for the tables?" I asked.

"No, not as yet," she returned.

"That sounds perfect for the color scheme. Why don't you do that?" she offered, and then drifted away somewhat disinterested.

The wedding approached. That day I carefully washed and shined my crystal goblets as rainbows of light played to them from my sunny window. How very beautiful they were and how lovely the arrangements would look. I cut slips of flowers from my garden and carefully fashioned lovely centerpieces. Later I took them to the church, and I was met with hearty approval of how beautiful they were.

After a beautiful candlelight wedding in the sanctuary, the wedding party convened in the basement annex for the reception. Hurrying through the line, I was anxious to see how the tables looked. As we moved forward, I gasped in horror. Cascading in interesting patterns from the crystal goblets was only fern-like foliage—no blossoms anywhere.

"What has happened to my arrangements?" I gasped innocently to no one in particular.

A woman next to me offered sympathetically, "You didn't know? Moss rose always closes at dusk."

If you are irritated by every rub,

how can you be polished?
—Rumi

My Little Shell

I'm in my little shell.
   Occasionally I peek out
      When no one is around.

Sharp words put me here—
   Angry accusations
      False insinuations.

Someday I'll come out,
   But give me a little time
      For I must rest a while.

It's very dark in here.
   The light comes only
      Through small cracks.

I can't move around too well,
   And it's getting
      A little stuffy.

Lying on my back
    Makes the ridges of my shell
        Gouge.

As do angry words—
    Pointed accusations
        Sharp insinuations.

I must leave
    Before I get stiff
        And cold

With dampness in my soul
    From the tears
        I have cried.

But look:
    The tears have washed
        As angry waves refine.

And all my fine abrasions—
    Will they someday result
        In a pearl?

The Rose

Felecia stamped as she whirled away from the water fountain, tossing her long, brownish hair just to make a point. "Did you see what she did? That new girl is just pushy and selfish. She won't last two months. You don't put huge signs on the outside of the lobby to announce your shop opening without even clearing it with the manager! What nerve?! Who does she think she is?"

She took a long drag on a slim-line cigarette and then snapped a sparkling silver lighter shut as she blew smoke nowhere in particular. Her hand, with its blood-red long nails, expertly placed the cigarette pack neatly in her purse. High heels clicking, she made her way back from the lounge area to her desk, a too-short tropical skirt accommodating her determined gait.

Felicia was a veteran concierge at a beachfront resort in Hawaii, nearing retirement. Her smooth dialogue could sell air-conditioners to Alaskans in the dead of winter if need be, and she was fine to work with as long as you didn't invade her territory. If you did—look out!

I returned to my studio without comment. Felicia had definite opinions and really didn't care what anybody else thought.

Just then the bouncy, petite newcomer just mentioned came into view. Betsy was a bundle of energy with an outgoing disposition. Nodding in Felicia's direction, she stopped and positioned her near-perfect figure to place another large sign for her new business in the lobby to complement the one on the front lawn. It was a little too close to the connoisseur's desk.

"I'm allergic to cigarette smoke. Did you know that?" Betsy threw at Felicia while fingering her curly updo absentmindedly. "I get violently ill when anyone smokes in the same room."

I could almost feel the vibrations from my studio. Turning quickly, Betsy looked my way and waved. I hesitantly returned the gesture, while rearranging a shelf. Betsy then went about the task of placing artful displays in her coffee shop window, seemingly oblivious to the fact that she had stepped on someone's toes big-time. Soon I could hear the loud clicking of high heels making determined steps to the manager's office. The door shut firmly.

21

Unfortunately things didn't improve in the next several weeks, and I seemed to have acquired the position of complaint department, counselor, and mediator. My studio was a little too close to the conflict.

"Her prices are sooo out of reason, I always got my coffee for half the price when Tony ran the shop," Felicia, the drama queen, said one day in her throaty voice. She failed to mention the fact that she was indulging in a double cappuccino from Betsy's shop instead of a regular cup of coffee from Tony.

After such comments, Betsy would fly into my studio, upset because Felecia's voice was too loud and droning or Felicia reeked of smoke.

Felecia became more discreet with her complaining. A veteran in tourism, she knew the consequences of constant strife among the staff. Her digs at Betsy became more casual and off the cuff rather than saturated with out-and-out distain.

Needless to say, the cold war continued. "Have you heard the news?" Betsy gleefully volunteered one day in the lobby.

"What news?" I asked.

"One of Felicia's coworkers said she is having trouble on the job. She can be difficult, you know. Frankly, I think her time is limited."

"Oh, it's probably just a rumor," I said, though I knew that the situation was getting ugly.

After mulling the situation for a while, I decided, *Why not try a little peacemaking experiment?*

After work, I went to the nearest florist and purchased a long-stem rose. Using my key to the side door after the last employee had left, I entered the vacant lobby and carefully placed the rose in a vase on Felicia's desk. I retreated softly, closed the door behind me, and quietly left.

The next day, when I came to open my studio, Felecia was trying to find the source of her beautiful rose. I wasn't a suspect, for I closed in the evening while others were still there, not to return until everyone's shift had begun the next morning.

"Are you sure someone didn't deliver this last evening after I left?" Felicia eagerly asked the desk clerk again.

"No. No one came as long as the desk was open," replied the clerk.

There was only one person who came in earlier than the rest to get the coffee going, and that was Betsy. But no one dared suggest Betsy had left the rose. Betsy was appalled. I could imagine her turmoil: someone sent Felicia a beautiful rose—the woman with the droning voice, the women who couldn't live without her cigarettes, the woman pushing retirement whose too-short dresses were exasperating?

As I went on errands for my studio that week, I passed the beautiful rose occasionally. Its fragrance filled the lobby as it graced a prominent place at the center of Felicia's desk. She seemed so proud to display it, perhaps as an affirmation of her worth.

The delicate presence lasted a full week, and with the presence the atmosphere began to change. In the weeks that followed, Felicia began treating Betsy less abruptly. Betsy became less critical of Felicia. Finally they began having amicable conversations.

Nothing more was said of the rose. Though it was eventually discarded, its fragrance remained.

My Dollies Three

A little girl in saucy curls
Had three china dolls one day,
And she lined them up upon a shelf
To view the fine array.

As she stood by to admire
Her lovely friends with glee
She slipped upon a rug nearby
Jarring the set of three.

Tears of sorrow filled her eyes
As she realized what she'd done.
For Rebecca, Ruth and Emily
Lay broken in the sun.

She picked them up so tenderly.
"Father," she called, "Come see!
You must mend my broken pieces.
You must fix them like new for me."

24

Father looked the situation over
And quietly went about
Placing carefully piece by piece
Renewing hope, not doubt.

And when the task was finished,
Each piece carefully glued in place.
The little girl cried, "But, Daddy!
There are scars upon each face?"

"My child the pieces were broken.
They can never be the same.
But you still have your friends, you know,
And can call them each by name."

The little girl turned in sorrow.
"My carelessness," she cried,
"Has caused such grief and heartache
To my dollies, side by side."

But the story ends not in sorrow
Nor should there be dismay.
There's bright hope for each tomorrow
As we heed lessons then obey.

You see, each of us through carelessness
May jar another's way.
We may shatter one unintentionally
By a thoughtless deed one day.

Then we must gather the remnants of sorrow
And take them to the Master's hand.
There will be no more grief to borrow.
Through forgiveness, we'll understand.

Scars need not be remaining.
Restoration can be ours.
For you see the One sent from heaven;
He forever bears our scars.

A Recipe for Friendship

Take a bit of thoughtfulness
As you journey through each day.

Add a little kindness
Here and there along the way.

Laughter too, will make life richer,
Make it light and so supreme.

And don't forget "Congratulations"
To one whose realized a dream.

A cup brimming full of gladness
Will add a sparkle too.

So be happy to serve others
With the best that you can do.

Add sympathy gently, when needed,
And encouragement do share,

When one you know is troubled
'Neath a load of pain or care.

Kind words take but a moment
And will gain much in the end.

For you see these are ingredients
For the making of a friend.

Growth and Adventure

God opens millions of flowers
Without forcing the buds.
It reminds us not to force anything
For things happen at the right time.

—Unknown

Geranium Grandeur

The blooms are exquisite, with splotches of velvety red against lush green leaves. These geranium plants I had nurtured with care to produce continual blooms for my garden. Now healthy look alike blooms were my pride and joy. Exiting through the garden gate, I notice buds from my sturdy plants pushing through the slats of the garden fence, and some were blooming happily on the outside of the garden. *Couldn't stay put, had to find new territory to explore,* I mused

Growing geraniums sort of reminds me of growing a family I mused one day A family produces a continuous line—like the variety of my red geraniums—similar, yet not the same. A family requires strong roots-- the result of tender nurturing, as did my healthy, red geraniums waving in the breeze. And families experience expansion, when young members wish to explore new territory as did the geranium buds pushing with determination through the slatted fence. This can be healthy, when exploring brings new areas of productivity to their lives.

We had given our blessing as our children embarked on career pathways suited just for them and soon our family would welcome a new son and daughter through a double wedding to would take place in late summer. Yes, our son and daughter each had selected new territories.

So we embrace change, and while doing so remember that change is inevitable and with change come new adventures. Exploration and adventure can keep us from the doldrums of life. Let's embrace change with a proper perspective for others and ourselves.

The Summons

It's funny how children bend toward their destiny at a very early age. At the age of three, our daughter insisted on carrying trays to her grandmother, who was at our home for a short convalescence. Laura is now a nurse.

Our son loved being outdoors and around animals. At an early age, he seemed drawn toward caring for them. He became manager of the swine division of our farming operation.

When I entered first grade, my teacher got my number quickly. "Just put Dee in a play, and she'll be happy," she would say with a smile. She saw to it that I played Goldilocks when we did *The Three Bears* for the other classes in our school. I'm sure she also found the strengths of each child she taught and encouraged them in the area that was right for them. That was just the kind of person she was.

As I progressed through elementary and high school, my favorite teachers were always the music teachers. The ones we had were quite young, and I marveled how they seemed to glide in and lead us in songs and plays so perfectly.

Someday, I mused, *I'm going to be a music teacher.* However, I put my dream aside, married my true love, and began raising two wonderful children, until one day …

The telephone rang insistently, and I hid my head under the pillow. It was Monday morning, and my children had just left on the school bus. I had crawled back into bed to rest from hosting an extended-family gathering over the weekend. Finally, when the ringing wouldn't stop, I got up and wearily answered it.

"Good morning, Dee." It was the secretary of the local elementary school.

"Good morning" was my hardly audible reply.

"We're having a little problem here and are hoping you can help us out."

"Oh? What's the problem?" My interest was quickened. Had something happen with the children?

"Now, don't be alarmed," she continued. "Our music teacher is having difficulty with severe leg pain. Her doctor has told her to take some time off. We've search and searched through our substitutes list, but no one wants to do music. Would you, by any chance, be interested in filling in for a while?"

The question hit me right between the eyes. No longer was I dreary-eyed and half awake. I had no teaching certificate—only the accumulated experience with my musical family in performances at civic and church functions and some teaching in Sunday school. I was flabbergasted. But before I knew it, I was agreeing to go that morning and help them out.

I forgot my weariness as the excitement to pursue a new adventure took over. I threw on what I thought was my best teaching apparel and left a note on the kitchen table for my husband when he came in for lunch: "GONE TO TEACH SCHOOL!" I knew that would raise his eyebrows a bit.

Thus was my introduction to a career in education.

The next two weeks found me driving between three schools in the area to teach elementary music. I soon found that I had many songs and ditties I could pull out of my sleeve to keep the students involved. Plus, I was having a ball.

I thought, *Perhaps the abandoned dream stuffed down deep inside me as a little girl might become a reality. Could this be an open door?* With time on my hands and both children in school, I enrolled in college that January.

It's funny how little things spur you on once you've decided on a goal. Since I had been out of high school for ten years, I had to take the SAT test. Fine. I signed up to take it on a November day and then spent many hours studying.

The exam day arrived, and I eagerly started for my destination. The journey exhilarated me with expectancy until about three-fourths of a mile from the exam center, I had a flat. What to do? There was no time to see about a repair, and to hike the rest of the way would make me late. I just had to make that appointment, so I rolled on and came to a parking place in the front of the test center with the tire flapping. What a mess! I lamented as I stopped to survey the damage and mentally assess the cost. Students milling around the front, waiting for the same exam, looked on.

Nevertheless, I brushed past my dilapidated tire rim to attend to the job at hand. I later learned my scores did not indicate a shining career in education. However after completing two majors—elementary and music—and receiving an administrator's degree, I had disregarded their implication.

One of my first teaching assignments after college was in a small town near the Wabash River. The summer before school was to convene in the fall, I strolled into the stark, bare music room in the very old elementary building after my interview with the band director. On the blackboard was written *I HATE MUSIC*. I guess it was a final contribution of one of the students before leaving for summer vacation.

I surveyed a dusty, old bookcase of music books that surely were at least forty years old, for they were raveling at the seams.

I was also told soon afterward that there were no textbooks for the two sections of junior high music classes with nearly thirty students I was responsible for in addition to all the elementary classes. I was also informed that there would be no principal in the building, for he divided his position between the elementary and high schools, so I was pretty much on my own in the area of discipline. The elementary music classes would be no problem, but what would I do with two classes of thirty active junior high students for fifty minutes five days a week with absolutely no teaching material?

My first conversation with the principal-at-large was very informative. He said, "One year, we didn't have a music teacher, so I just put on the Christmas program myself!"

What caliber of programs are the people expecting? I wondered. "Well, the sky's the limit!" I said.

I encountered one very bright sixth-grader, the son of the local tavern owner, who volunteered his insights about six weeks after school had taken up. "I know every teacher on this staff that smokes." Then he began naming each one. Well, he had us all pegged already. I wasn't on his list.

The year turned out pretty successful, despite the fact I was asked to stop having our first- and second-graders march to upbeat music, because the ceiling below had started to fall.

Oh yes, and our very creative Christmas pageant with skits and colorful costuming ended on a note of unintentional hilarity. For one of our skits, a tack was purposely left on a chair at the end. I had asked one of the high school faculty, who also was a pastor, to end our program with a devotional on the real meaning

of Christmas. I had assumed he would return to his seat in the audience afterward. Instead, forgetting the previous program content, he chose to sit on the nearest convenient chair. *The one with the tack on it!* I can still hear the student body saying, *"Humph!"* as he sat down.

Continuing Education from the Small

Misinformed?

The kindergarten class had just finished music time. We had been singing many of the nursery rhymes that the students loved so much. One of the last songs was "Mary Had Little Lamb." As the children filed past me at the door, one pert little blonde with corkscrew curls stopped short and announced her new discovery: "I didn't know fleas were white."

Service with a Smile

"Hi, Mom," called my six-year-old bundle of brown curls and blue eyes as she bounced off the school bus and into the kitchen. "Want a sandwich with me?"

"Sure, why not" came my absentminded reply. I was finishing the work on a school assignment before taking a break. A fleeting thought momentarily crossed my mind as to just what interesting concoction might appear. Laurie was known to come up with rather strange recipes.

I listened as my pert second-grader hummed happily as she busied herself in the kitchen, whisking first from the refrigerator to the cupboard. Soon a sandwich carefully placed on a plate appeared on my desk. She smiled brightly, her cheeks dimpled, then plopped down beside me to enjoy her sandwich as well.

I bit into mine, then stopped short. "Oh Laurie!" I managed. "Jelly with *pickles* on top?"

My Country 'Tis of Thee?

He brushed his dark hair to the side, his big, solemn dark eyes flecked with interest. It was music time, and he took his seat with the usual anticipation. A quiet, sensitive lad, Randy loved music. His favorite time was when students could request a special song to sing at the end of the period. Randy's request was always "My Country 'Tis of Thee."

Patriotic songs were always encouraged, so often Randy's wish was granted. He then would revel in each word. By the end of the year, he seemed to have memorized the first and last verses, although learning did not come easy for him.

34

Meanwhile the country had erupted in controversy over the questionable conduct of our president. It was the topic of conversation everywhere, given priority in news reports. Sure enough, at request time, Randy raised his hand and innocently asked, "Can we sing 'My Country's Tired of Me'?"

Robin

She sat there silently, head bent down. Little tears had made blobs and smears on the lined paper where she was learning to write her name. I tried to soothe her, saying, "It's all right. We'll just start again." I tore the sheet off her tablet so she could use a fresh one.

"Now, let's begin."

"But I just keep making too many accidents," was her solemn reply.

Chicken Anyone?

We live in the Midwest. It's farming country, a land of waving cornfields and neat rows of soybeans with a few spots of golden wheat. There isn't much entertainment in rural areas—very few concerts or art galleries for stimulation—so we must create our own. Sometimes it is just all in good fun.

One Sunday afternoon, my husband and I started out on our bikes to visit a couple about three miles down the road. We had grown up with these two, and our families visited often, so we thought we'd just drop in. When we got there, they were gone, so my husband, being the mischievous character he is, pulled a large stalk of corn from the field near the driveway, opened their mailbox, and pushed it in root first—with all the clumped dirt—leaving the rest dangling. This was to let them know someone had come to call.

Several days later, we had heard nothing from our neighbors and had almost forgotten my husband's little gesture when a horn blasted from our front drive. It was the mailman pulling in.

"Miss," he managed as he got out of the car with a puzzled grin when I came running out. "Did you know you had a chicken in your mailbox?"

"A chicken?!" I gasped in astonishment. "What kind of a chicken?"

"A very messy one, Miss. Someone put it in head first. It's still alive. I think it has been there a while. Here's your mail for today. I'll let you attend to the other delivery." With that he smiled brightly and headed for his car.

Well, I had known it was coming, so I had an idea who the comic was who had made our special delivery. I transported a weary but squawking chicken to a nearby coop for safekeeping. And cleaning the mailbox with the garden hose was no desirable task.

"Hmm, we'll see about this," I mumbled with a grin.

Two weeks later I made a friendly phone call to our neighbors. "Bill, we haven't seen you folks in a while," I began innocently. "I wonder if you'd come up for an evening meal one night this week. You're not too busy now, since the crops are growing, are you?"

"No, no, just a minute. I'll check with Harriet." He said a moment later, "She said we're free. We'd be glad to come."

"Would Friday evening work for you, about six thirty?"

"Sure, Friday evening would be fine. By the way, what's for supper?"

Did I detect a note of hesitancy in his voice? "Oh, I'll think of something. We'll look forward to having you come."

"Sure, thanks for the invite."

This should be fun, I thought, hanging up the phone. Of course, no mention of either incident had been made, and I was sure he was wondering if we had found the chicken.

Wednesday came around, and I killed and dressed the fatted chicken for our evening meal. I figured I might as well use it all. I prepared a lettuce and tomato salad and sprinkled chicken feathers in it for Bill's plate, along with fried chicken, mashed potatoes and gravy, and fresh green beans from the garden.

Friday at six thirty rolled around, and our two friendly neighbors came in. Joyous greetings and happy laughter occurred, as it did every time we got together. But Bill seemed a bit on guard.

We settled down to the table, and after prayers (Of course, I breathed, "Lord, forgive me"), I served the salad. It was such fun when Bill finally realized after a few bites and spits that he had more in his salad than he had bargained for. He looked at me, puckering. "I know! You don't have to explain!" he bellowed with a grin.

"Well, now," I said. "I didn't want to waste any part of that good chicken someone left in my mailbox." The group at the table convulsed in laughter.

"All right, you win!" he managed.

I produced another salad for Bill, and he was finally able to eat in peace.

Our chicken story made the rounds in our small community for some time. It was certainly one of the highlights of our mail carrier's career.

Nuff said!

Your wrinkles either show that you are nasty, cranky, and senile
or that you're always smiling.

—Carlos Santana

Garage Sale Today!

I peeked out my front window. There sat a pickup truck across the street, awaiting the kill. More cars and trucks began to descend, and it was only 7:15 a.m. The garage door wasn't to go up until eight. Promises must be kept to prospective buyers: "No Early Sales!"

Just then my mother-in-law slid in the side door armed with the moneybox and additional tags. "Where do these go?" she whispered, gesturing wildly, so as not to start a riot among the people lined in front of my garage door.

"Just put them on the table." I did a couple of last-minute tasks, trying to appear calm, collected, and braced for the descending mob. Then, with all in order, I made a brash and reckless movement: I pushed the garage door button. It obligingly ascended to reveal a ménage of powerful, determined looks.

Three people encircled my maple dinette, pointed, and said, "I want that!"

"She spoke first!" I managed apologetically, kicking myself because I had failed to price it high enough. But then, although they looked very nice yet, I'd had to glue those chairs together on a regular basis for the last five years. I hoped the stout woman who won the argument would keep up the procedure—or she might be sitting on the floor instead of a chair in a month or so.

"A real steal," I heard her whisper to her friend.

"Well, I've made someone happy today," I rationalized under my breath.

People do strange things at garage sales. Large, stately women try on petite clothes. Friends of many years cart off forty-dollar chairs for only ten dollars. Loving neighbors give you their best wares to sell for them, just to increase your volume. And husbands become distraught with all "this foolishness" of putting up racks and carting tables around.

"What's your problem?" I blasted at my husband as I sipped coffee from a four-cornered cup that he had picked up in a bunch of things at a farm auction.

"A real steal," he had boasted. "I got all of this for a quarter."

Included in the odd assortment was a replica of a cannibal, as part of the family had been missionaries in Africa at one time.

"Did you ever try to drink from a four-cornered cup?" I asked. "Well, someone else did, and that's why we got them." I washed out the cup and put it out for sale.

"You certainly learn a lot by having a garage sale," I lamented a week later, as I counted to ten, waiting to see if my newly acquired toaster would throw the toast or burn it. I'd exchanged it with a neighbor for the four-cornered cups. She thought they were quite a novelty and would go wonderful with her unique teapot. She then convinced me that her toaster would be a marvelous addition to my kitchen.

"I should never have listened," I declared as I caught the toast as it went sailing by.

Later I noticed some pretty white materials among the leftover items. *These curtains might look nice in the bathroom for a change,* I thought, as I swished them around gaily. Turning to the line of clothes left over in the garage, I discovered a suit coat I had found in a bargain basement, but I had never gotten around to getting anything to match it. I had seen one similar to it in Macy's window a few days before. I thought, *Maybe I'll just take it to town and find materials to sew a skirt.*

As I finished the last of the cleaning up and went into the house, I noticed something sticking on my finger. I peeled off a round piece of tape and read, "Size 9–10 @ $2.00." And I thought, *Two dollars is about all my husband would take for me about now.*

Then I mused, *Gosh, I need a break. I think I'll take the extra cash and go shopping.*

Create

My husband moans
    With words and phrases,
Participles and clauses—

Not accents and periods—
Of interior design,
    Carpets and drapes,
To change and refine.

Words are wise.
Words are enlightening.
    And the expense, my dear,
Is by far less frightening!

Perseverance

The wedding was fast approaching. Our son and daughter and their future spouses had decided to repeat their vows in a double wedding ceremony. It would be in August, only three months away, in a lovely setting outside our little church just down the road. The reception would follow immediately in our yard and pool area.

It was such an adventure to be a part of this special event. We prepared happily to accommodate our guests.

One day we were cleaning our yard and patio when my husband called to me, "Did you plant these?"

I ambled over to see what he was talking about, only to find on both sides of the sidewalk, near our patio entry, two little volunteer marigold plants starting to stretch bravely upward to the sun. "No, I didn't plant them, but let's just leave them. They might add some welcoming color for our guests." He carefully mulched the soil around them so they would thrive.

As the days progressed, I found myself caught up in endless activities to prepare for this unique event. Since three families were involved, multiple decisions had to be made to make our occasion an enjoyable experience for all.

The wedding was to be in front of the church in a large raised area surrounded by a stone wall at the church entry. The crowd would be seated a little below. It was a perfect setting, since the church was too small to house the families and friends, but the yard outside would make a lovely setting.

To accommodate the crowd, our neighbor, Bob, who lived across the road from the church, had graciously volunteered to handle the parking, using his place as well as the church grounds to accommodate the cars.

Millions of thoughts flitted through my mind about the preparations that must be made. *How many should be invited? What if it rains?* I could envision car motors racing in mud puddles to get parked as strains of wedding music soared.

Selecting bridal attire and planning a color scheme was fun filled, but then came the worry.

Hectic telephone calls had to be made to change last-minute plans. Invitation lists needed to be prepared for prenuptial showers and the wedding day. Catering decisions for the wedding meal that the Ladies Aid would serve had to be finalized. … On and on it went.

One day my husband exclaimed, "Why all this fuss—for something that will take only one day?"

I strolled to the patio for a breath of fresh air. Beside the walk, I discovered the almost forgotten marigolds stretching majestically as if they had a mission all their own. As the late-summer buds began to form on the tender plants, it seemed they too were preparing for the day, while waving nonchalantly in the breeze. I watched their continued progress with interest as dresses were altered, bridesmaid shoes were matched, and the bouquets were finally chosen.

Oh, to be as carefree as my marigolds, I thought as I notice tiny dots of yellow near the marigolds' bud tips.

Finally the hectic pace subsided, and the wedding day dawned beautiful and clear. All last-minute errands behind us, we would now walk to the church so visible from our yard. I breathed a prayer of gratitude. Why had I worried? Didn't I realize that this special event was in hands bigger than my own, as my little marigold messengers suggested? Pausing at the patio steps before we left for the church, I noticed that the nodding little buds had burst into full, summer bloom as if to say, "See, I told you so."

"Consider how the lilies grow. They do not labor or spin..."
Luke 12:27

Lessons by the Sea

Anchored in God

I get up at six, grab a cup of coffee, and head for the beach. It is so quiet and peaceful here. I watch huge turtles nipping at the surface in the grayness of early morning. I stoop to pick up bright coral and white rocks for my collection in the golden urn by my door. Sometimes trade winds blow, and my golden urn goes bouncing

down from its sturdy shelf. But little by little, the weight of my rocks and coral will anchor it, as I carry a few back with me each morning.

I also feel anchored as I spend the first moments of the day in the beauty of God's creation. Adoration of all He is and ever will be steadies me and prepares me for the day He has given.

The sun just lit the little resort up the shore. A faint rainbow is trying to appear, as sprinkles of rain brush my face.

It has been good to start the day in this quietness.

Sand

The sand is continually shifting, ever pliable to the waves. How flexible it is; first it ripples, then mounds, adjusting to the elements around.

Sand protects, covers, absorbs, and brings comfort and beauty as the sun glints, shimmering from beige to white. However, in the wrong place, sand can be abrasive: between your toes, in tight shoes, or around your face. How necessary to be in the right place. How disturbing to be in the wrong.

We have purpose too. How fulfilling when we find it.

An Unexpected Swish

It always amuses me to watch vacationers who come to the beach for the first time. They watch with fascination as the waves gently roll in and cover their feet with a cleansing wash. After standing and enjoying the gentle foot bath, they take their beach chairs and sit near the water, where they can enjoy the gentle, occasional lapping over their feet.

All of a sudden, a big wave comes splashing in and covers not only their feet, but almost everything else. I'm convinced, after watching this happen many times, that the sea must have a sense of humor and is enjoying the run.

The visitors then sit, spluttering and shaking the sand off as they get up much wiser and move their chairs. Some laugh it off and make the best of the situations. Others are clearly irritated and run for escape.

I cannot help but muse about how life can bring big waves of unwelcomed problems when we are only hoping for a little pleasure. We are conditioned to expect the best for ourselves: As we check out at the grocery store, the friendly cashier leaves us with, "Have a good day." Or we hear when we are put on hold, "Your call is *very important* to us."

Life, however, cannot be all self-gratification. If it were, we would become spoiled beyond words. No, there must be a balance as we learn to take the good with the bad, and it's the way we handle the unexpected waves that determines our destiny. Will we make the best of what comes? Or will we let the waves of life cause us to run for escape?

Gray Days of Opportunity

Today the ocean is gray. There is a continual beating of waves back and forth over black jagged rocks in a slow, regular duple meter. Not one of the most exciting days to be on the beach—no sun, no fun. But look! I see a boy of sixteen touching a rock to end a long journey down the beach. Perhaps he is preparing for a marathon. Two birds flutter near a tree, building a nest to raise a family. A little boy and girl, shovels and pails in hand, industriously fashion a large sand castle.

We create a promising future when the sun will shine, by the strides we make on mundane days?

Colorful Capers!

From seemingly nowhere, a giant paint brush has dotted the sea with splashes of yellow, pinks, orange, lavenders, and rich green as windsurfers bob up and down on the ocean of blue.

They zoom in an out, trying to avoid collisions on a journey to they know not where. What fun to see where they land! Occasionally they tumble, but right themselves and soon are on their way. Others lie sprawling.

What delight! What madness! There must be a hundred amid the turbulence.

Where are they going? Nowhere.

What are they doing? Just trying to stay afloat,

But darting to and fro is fun. There is color! There is excitement!

Life can be like that, too, with the colorful madness of reacting to a whim.

Sprawling, getting up, but going nowhere in particular. Color and excitement can be deceiving.

Is my voyage carefully taken? Do I value opportunities as they come my way, or am I just here for the ride?

The Storm

Angry waves roar as the storm presses vehemently against the shoreline, pounding deep crevices into a once smooth rock formation. What power its lashes thrust upon the rock. Experience tells me the rock formation and sand will be changed somewhat over a period of time by the beating and whipping of the angry sea.

My eyes turn away to focus on a little fishing ship, out in the hurling sea. It is trying to make its way through the storm after a seemingly successful fishing voyage. The ship's course is set, as it moves bravely on. My eyes follow as it reaches the distant harbor, thrashed by angry waves, but not destroyed. I marveled at its determination.

We too must press through storms. Some are of our own making, while others are thrust upon us by circumstances. Those storms change us, sometimes carving new crevices into our once secure foundations. They may toss us around, challenging the very existence of our faith, but they are teachers, and their lessons carve out an understanding that we might never have known had we not experienced them.

> When the storms of life are raging, stand by me;
> When the storms of life are raging, stand by me.
> When the world is tossing me, like a ship upon the sea,
> Lord who rules the wind and water, stand by me.

—C. A. Tindley

The Flower-Garden Quilt

Hugh flakes of snow fell silently, teasing flushed cheeks as Michael and I made our way from the barn. As he trudged thoughtfully, his small steps keeping pace with Mommy's longer gait, my son's tumbling locks beneath a cap of whiteness were drenched with winter froth. He shook vehemently before entering the warmth of our farmhouse.

"Will the thigs be safe under the heating lamp, Mommy?" he asked anxiously, unable to pronounce *pigs*.

"Of course. They are now snug and warm and will be able to nurse and grow strong away from the winter's cold.

Although my answer was calm and reassuring, my state of mind wasn't. I unwrapped my swollen body and helped my tow-headed son with his layers of coats, boots, and soggy mittens. Our second child was to arrive in late March, and we had hardly begun January. It had been a difficult pregnancy. The days seemed to wear on as if the colors of my life disappeared into a cloak of winter gray. Silent walls screamed at me as the days of not feeling well took their toll.

I glanced at a lush green plant nestled next to the kitchen counter, safely below the icy windowpane. I had hoped that it would produce some color to signify the coming of a brighter day. Mother had given it to me in the fall, saying it was an impatiens. She had brought it in from her garden so it would not freeze. "Water it and feed it with plant food, and it will bloom brightly again," she said. But its response to that care was a colorless existence along with mine.

"*Impatiens*, sounds like *impatient*, which is exactly what I am."

Just then the ringing of the phone caught my attention.

The soft voice on the other end of the line was Aunt Ina's, a great-aunt who lived down the road. "Would you like a flower-garden quilt to work on these winter months?" she offered after we had talked awhile.

"Well, that's nice of you but—"

"Friends around gave me their scraps of material so I would have enough pieces to finish this quilt, but my eyesight simple is not what it used to be. I know I will not be able to finish it." Perhaps she sensed that I might need something to help pass the long, monotonous days of winter.

I recalled having watched my mother quilt when I was a child, as she took on various projects for the church missionary group. But I had attempted only one small quilt, which was for our son before he was born. Piecing a flower-garden quilt with its hexagon design seemed a bit much for a novice like me. However, Aunt Ina was convinced I was up to the task.

A few days later, I was piecing the quilt, enjoying its bright hues. There were so many pieces, I wondered if I would ever get it done. Michael rolled his tractor along the border of our living room rug while, piece by piece and stitch by stitch, I wore the days away.

Soon I discovered a splendid design of purple in the array of colors before me. It looked like something Aunt Ina's grandaughter Louise might wear. Yes, I was sure I had seen her wear it to worship. Louise had left the community and become an award-winning teacher in a larger city. What an inspiration she was to her family and community!

Another day, I discovered a chambray denim. How like Hallie this one was. After surviving cancer, she and her husband had been involved in a car accident that had left him a paraplegic. Yet she had gathered the courage to develop a fine, producing farm, and they both engaged in many activities to help the handicapped. *She must have had many gray days,* I thought, chiding myself.

By then, I had brought the little impatiens to sit beneath the east window beside my rocker, where I carefully cut designs and tried to imagine what material had been given by whom.

As I stitched a rose print, my memory traveled to the time of Aunt Rebecca's passing. Her family had come home for Christmas Eve gathering, and she had died peacefully during the night after their departure.

That Christmas morning, a car drove into our driveway. Looking out, I saw her husband getting out of his car. Having made arrangements for her burial, he thought it necessary to distribute the gifts she had made for others weeks before her passing.

"These people around me are the salt of the earth," I exclaimed to no one in particular. What lessons in fortitude they teach.

Day after day I worked with the colors that sprang before me, sometimes telling sweet stories, sometimes relating the experiences of the people whose lives bore the threads of their existence. Then slowly the days became sunnier. Long icicles at my window dripped steadily to the barren flower bed below, and deep mounds of snow slipped quietly into swirling streams in the meadow beyond our gate.

One day I made the last stitch on the beautiful flower-garden quilt that was now my precious possession. *What colors will my life take?* I mused. *Will I yield to a monotonous gray, or will I take full responsibility for the decisions I make? Will I blend, stand out, adjust to life's threatening blows, and bloom in spite of it all?*

The day finally arrived for our baby to join our household. We hurried off to the hospital in the dawn light and later excitedly brought home a darling baby girl all bundled in pink. As we stepped into our living room, there by the rocker I spotted the lush impatiens. It was bright with brilliant blooms. Tears filled by eyes.

"Thank you, God," I murmured softly, "for the quilt to teach me lessons and quiet my nerves, and the little plant with its message of hope."

Good for the body is work of the body,
and good for the soul is the work of the soul
and good for either is the
work of the other.

—Thoreau

The Flower That Softly Spoke

A little flower grew one day
   Beside the garden wall.
    Just a small one, too,
     But bright each day,
      Blooming so fair for all.

I watched it there to see it bloom
   'Mid tangled vine and tare.
    I watched it sway
     With bitter winds,
      But it seemed so free of care.

I gazed when scorching sun bent low.
   I watched the raindrops fall.
    But the little flower
     Just bloomed on
      Beside the garden wall.

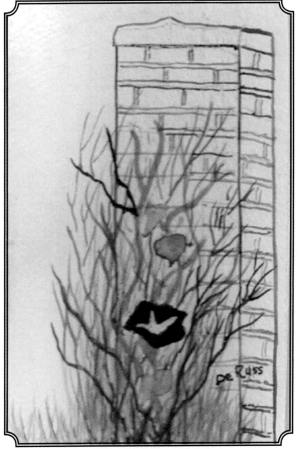

The sun grew dim; the earth grew cold.
My little flower was gone.
Then winter came
And a blanket of snow
Covered the once green lawn.

One day the earth awoke.
My steps were swift to see
The little flower by the garden wall.
Would it bloom again for me?

Then suddenly, before my eyes,
　　My breath caught at the wonder,
　　　　For a vast array of color
　　　　　Filled the wall
　　　　　　　With blooms asunder.

So if you're tired of blooming
　　And harsh winds bend you low.
　　　　　Just remember the little flower
　　　　　　And blooming on you'll go.

For God plants us
　　Where He needs us.
　　　　We must not question or complain.
　　We must not refuse to bloom
　　　In the cold and bitter rain.

And someday seeds will scatter
　　From the blooming you have done,
　　　　　Just like the little flower
　　　　　　　First blooming in the sun.

56

Hope

It is often in the darkest skies,
We see the brightest stars.

—Richard Evans

The Dogwood

The picture my kitchen window framed was breathtaking: huge blooms etched with pink and crowned with golden-yellow centers. We had welcomed this beauty every spring for many years, but it had not always been so.

Grandma had given each one of her grandchildren a flowering shrub in the last years of her life. Ours would be a pink dogwood. The gift was for both of us—my husband, Don, and me—as we shared birthdays in the month of June. We decided to plant our gift in a special place just outside our kitchen window, where it could be viewed easily from the kitchen and driveway.

Grandma would visit every once in a while from the neighboring town, where she lived in a little apartment. When she did, she would always check the little tree.

We cared for it, giving close attention, so it would flourish and grow, but time passed, and it did not bloom.

After a while, Grandma seemed discouraged by it and questioned her gift. We wondered if the place we'd selected for it was too shady.

Days became weeks, and weeks became months, and finally months turned into four years since we had been given our tree—and still no blossoms.

After a while, Grandma's health began to decline, and we lost her one December just before Christmas. The family gathered for Christmas giving that year, but Grandma and the enthusiasm that she always had as she presented her carefully selected gifts was sadly missed.

Day by day, winter finally turned into spring, with new life coming into bloom. One day we happened to see an unexpected bud on our little tree. We watched with interest as the tree began to awaken. Soon it stood before us encased in soft, radiant, pink blooms—Grandma's final gift.

The Dove

We traveled steadily northbound on a coastal road as it magically outlined the brilliant blues of Lake Michigan. Doilies of white splashes heaved insistently along our way as we traveled. I mentally dodged them, just as I'd been dodging the problems in my life the past days.

After deciding to get away for a while, my husband and I had left for a short vacation to this beautiful Michigan shoreline. As we drove northward, I clutched the chain of my shiny dove necklace. Putting the necklace on as we were leaving was perhaps an unconscious attempt to find peace in my soul. A dove—pure, docile—is a symbol of peace, a peace that I seemed to have lost in a flurry of family pressures but desperately needed to retrieve.

How does life suddenly tumble in on us? It can, with little or no warning, lash out with volumes of problems and no immediate answers, hurl storms of responsibilities with few results from our efforts, and carve deep sorrows for those we love but cannot seem to help?

My father was in the hospital for a lengthy stay, which greatly concerned our family. I had just thrashed through a hot summer, finishing a graduate school degree amid splashes of fun and frolic with our teenagers and their friends in our swimming pool.

My nerves were raw.

We meandered leisurely up the shoreline, looking for a place to stay for the night. Shortly we spotted a quaint little cabin perched on sand dunes, with willows waving an invitation to come.

"Yes, it can be ours for the night," said the owner, a salty sailor with a weatherworn hat.

With its rustic crudeness, the cabin was perfect. We immediately abandoned hot, sticky shorts and T-shirts for swimwear. I removed my dove necklace and placed it on the nightstand so I wouldn't lose it on the beach. We headed out into the brilliant blues and the softness of nature to bask in the redemptive elements of the shoreline.

We managed to stay another night in our cozy abode, but soon it was time to pack our things and move along. I reached for the dove necklace on the nightstand, but I could not find it.

"I'm sure I placed it here." I told my husband.

We searched on the floor, in drawers, through the sheets and all the bedding, but the dove wasn't to be found. We finally went on our way after telling the owner of the lost dove and asking if he would mail it to us should it be found.

We discovered other retreats during our meandering up the Michigan coastline. Gradually the warmth of the sun, gentle breezes, and the ribbon of blues from the soothing lakeshore began to revive our weary souls. The voice of the magnificent waters gave no direct answers to our problems, but in the vastness and splendor of nature came the healing.

I realized that there is One in control of all this beauty and magnitude. Even when harsh winds cause turbulence and roars of lashing waves beat vehemently, afterward a certain cleansing occurs.

As we began to load the car for our final trek homeward, I noticed a glint of silver on the floor near the door of our room. I slowly bent down to find there the jagged chain with its silver dove. *Where has it been?* I wondered. *This wasn't even where I lost it. How did it mysteriously get here?* Then a well-known biblical verse came to me: "Peace I leave with you, my peace I give you. I do not give as the world gives. Do not let your heart be troubled and do not be afraid." (John 14:27).

God's peace had never left, and the little dove was the evidence. Just like His peace, the dove had been there all along. I just needed to let go and accept it. I again placed the little dove, my symbol of peace, around my neck. We made our way home with renewed faith for the future.

Hope is the thing with feathers
That perches in the soul
And sings the tune
without the words
And never stops at all.

—Emily Dickinson

The Feathered Mates

They darted to and fro as the heavy blossoms of the dogwood tree hung obligingly, hiding their secret nest. Two dashes of red, one somewhat brighter than the other, flitted industriously around their emerging home.

I later peeked through the branches to see squawking mouths devour worm victims as the two faithfully hovered by protectively. Later, more flutters began emerging from a leafy green loft. Flying lessons were the order of the day, and the female encouraged awkward attempts as she fluttered here and there, urging them on.

Ever so soon, the little ones emerged, plump and confident, strutting on the lawn to investigate the world around.

One day, only too soon, the family disappeared, but life became very busy for me as I fulfilled teaching commitments and checked on my mother after Dad's recent passing.

I momentarily forgot my little friends, but after returning from school one afternoon, I noticed two redbirds sitting on a limb outside my window. "Family gone, empty nest," I mused.

As summer disappeared into a blaze of fall color, I saw the little male sitting all alone. He would fly away, then come back as if searching.

This seemed to be an afterschool ritual from then on, and I would see the little lonely bird fluttering around the tree. As fall approached, he did not leave, but often came and sat momentarily at my window. This continued for two years. My husband remarked how unusual for the little bird to stay around in cold weather.

That next July, Mother left us too, and I was also experiencing a vacancy in my life. We watched for our little red friend after that. Would he be company this year?

He never returned.

I believe that there is a subtle magnetism in Nature,
Which, if we unconscientiously yield to it, will direct us aright.

—Thoreau

63

A Rainbow of Promise

There's a beautiful rainbow at my window today—
A rainbow of promise for future array.

How brilliant its colors as it drops with the dew
To a mountain of stillness, of purple and blue.

Its splendor points to a quiet within
As I yield to the moment that whispers His plan.

Before I formed you in the womb, I knew …
But to know His purpose, we must listen and do.

Our dreams will be colored with shimmers of light,
Which could never be fathomed were we to recite.

And every so often, He reminds me again
By His rainbow of promise

I see now and then.

Just as nature passes through seasons, so do our lives move through warm springs and harsh winters. In soft whispers and nudges through different seasons of author Dee Russell's life, God has sometimes used the quietness of nature and the life of these colorful plants to speak to her, teaching valuable lessons that she sorely needed to learn. In the personal stories, paintings, and poetry of *The Flowers That Softly Spoke*, Russell now shares those lessons.

Reflection in the quiet environs of nature provides a secret to replenishing the spirit for the duties of the day, and this collection brings those reflections to life. Along the way, Russell considers relationships, growth and adventure, perseverance, and hope. These tales from her life outline the sometimes magical messages that flowers can offer and make clear the idea that we can choose the higher calling of listening to the still small voice within and searching out the wisdom of the scriptures that call us to a better way.

This illustrated inspirational collection presents anecdotes and verses designed to brighten your day with faith and friendship.

DEE RUSSELL and her husband, Don, spent their earlier years on a farm in the Midwest raising their family. Dee now teaches art and music to the children of Hawaii.

InspiringVoices®

Printed in the United States
By Bookmasters